Courage Within:
Indian Tales of Grit and Values

Stories of Strength, Character & Wisdom

Dr. SUSHANT RAJPUT

PUBLISHERS

Courage Within: Indian Tales of Grit and Values

First Edition:

Published by,
Mark-Fly Publishers
Coimbatore, Tamil Nadu.
www.markflypublishers.com
E-mail: info@markflypublishers.com,
markflypublishers@gmail.com

Cover Design & Typeset by :
Sanjay Panchal, Mark-Fly Team.

Edited by:
Mark-Fly Team.

Printed and Bound in India.

ISBN : 978-81-977327-6-8

Preface

Every book begins with a question.

Sometimes, it's one we ask ourselves.

Other times, it comes from someone we least expect.

My first book began with a simple but urgent desire: to help Gen Z, young professionals and college students searching for the skills no classroom teaches. How do you manage money, time, stress, relationships, and careers with confidence? That book was my attempt to answer.

My second book stretched its arms wider, speaking to adults of all ages. It became a guide to tackling procrastination and overthinking, the invisible brakes that slow us down even when we know how to move forward.

The response to both humbled me. Every message, every reader who found value in those pages, reminded me why I write.

But this book, 'Courage Within' was born of a very different kind of question.

"Why don't you write a storybook for me? One I can learn something from?"

That was the gentle, honest voice of my niece, Dhanya.

Her words stayed with me. They reminded me that while my earlier books spoke to professionals and adults, there was a generation rising quietly before our eyes- the Alpha generation.

Children are navigating a world louder, faster, and more demanding than ever. If there was ever a time to bring back timeless values like grit, empathy, discipline, and integrity, through the magic of story, it was now.

And so, Courage Within: Indian Tales of Grit and Values was born.

This collection is crafted especially for 10- to 15-year-olds, but its heart beats for everyone who believes in the power of character. Whether you're a child discovering the world or a grown-up rediscovering your roots, these stories are for you.

You will travel through rooftops in Gujarat and gardens in Sikkim, witness bullock races in Maharashtra and classrooms in Andhra. Across 21 stories, you'll meet children who stumble, fail, and rise again. Children who ask difficult questions, who stand their ground, and who make the brave choice, even when no one is watching.

Many of these characters are inspired by real people I met in my travels. It includes vendors in Varanasi, schoolchildren in Himachal, retired artists in Tamil Nadu. Their struggles and smiles, their quiet strength and fleeting joys, they live in these pages.

And some of these stories? They belong to the first storyteller I ever knew, my grandmother.

As a child, I would curl up beside her, soaking in tales rich with wisdom yet wrapped in warmth. She never lectured, never preached. She simply told stories. And in doing so, she shaped me.

She once told me: "A good story doesn't just pass time, it passes values."

That line has stayed with me ever since. I hope this book carries that same spirit forward.

Courage Within is my attempt to build a bridge.

Between generations,

Between old values and young hearts,

Between the reader you are and the person you're becoming.

Because courage doesn't always roar. Sometimes it sits quietly in your decisions, in how you treat others, in how you rise after a fall, in how you choose what's right even when it's hard.

To the young, the young-at-heart, and the storytellers among us: May these tales give you something to hold on to, and something worth passing on.

As you journey with Veer, Kavya, Gopal, Shanthi, and others, I hope their choices linger in your thoughts, sparking conversations long after the page is turned.

To make this book a living, breathing experience, I've also included chapter-wise activity sheets and a reflection journal designed to help readers pause, reflect, and apply each story's lessons in their own lives.

You can freely access these resources along with the resources that I had shared in my previous book at www.sushantrajput.co.in.

My hope is that Courage Within becomes less of a one-time read, and more of a modern-day Panchatantra for our times.

Acknowledgements

Some books begin with an idea. This one began with a question from my niece, Dhanya.

That question became the spark that lit a path I hadn't walked before. Dhanya, this book exists because of you. Your wide-eyed wonder, your thoughtful questions, and your hunger to grow. May these pages remind you that you already carry within you all the courage, kindness, and clarity you will ever need.

To the first storyteller of my life, my grandmother. Sitting at her feet, I learned that a story well-told is a lesson well-lived. Some morals in this book echo her voice; others are directly borrowed from her tales. Thank you, Ajji, for teaching me that values are not taught, they are passed down.

To my parents, who showed me the quiet strength of humility and the steady courage of consistency. And to my teachers, who sharpened my mind and gave me the tools to question and understand. Thank you for being the architects of my moral compass.

To my friends and family, whose everyday actions, whether late-night debates, words of encouragement, or unwavering faith, left their imprint on these stories. In your kindnesses and convictions, I found pieces of these characters.

To the countless people I met across India, the chai vendors in railway stations, the children waiting for buses, the weavers in villages, the elderly storytellers in temple courtyards, your stories live on here.

You may never know the impact you had, but your honesty, struggles, and resilience stitched themselves into these pages.

This collection is not just mine. It is a mosaic of voices, a fabric of values, woven together with love, laughter, struggle, and hope.

And finally, to my Mahadev, for the grace to walk this path and the blessing to share these stories.

To every reader, young and old, May you discover your own courage within.

Author Profile

Dr. Sushant Rajput

Dr. Sushant Rajput is a **two-time Amazon Bestselling Author**, **TEDx Speaker**, corporate leader, and educator with over **two decades of experience** across the IT, financial services, and consulting industries. He currently serves as **Vice President at eClerx Services Ltd.**, where he manages business development, while continuing his lifelong commitment to mentoring students and young professionals.

An alumnus of one of India's most respected business schools - KIMS, Dr. Rajput's professional journey is a story of reinvention, i.e. transitioning from **Computer Science** to **Investment Banking Operations**, moving into **Business Development**, and eventually emerging as an **Author, Faculty, and Thought Leader**.

Over the years, he has held various roles with organizations such as **HCL Technologies**, **Société Générale**, **Cognizant**, and **Deutsche Bank**. As a **Visiting Faculty and Corporate Mentor** at multiple management institutes, he actively guides MBA students on career readiness, emotional intelligence, professional ethics, and long-term personal development.

In recognition of his contributions to **education, literature, and youth development**, Dr. Rajput has been conferred with **two Honorary Doctorates**:

An **Honorary Doctorate in Humane Letters (Honoris Causa)** by the **World Human Rights Protection Commission (WHRPC)**, approved by the **Ministry of Skill Development & Entrepreneurship, Government of India**

An **Honorary Doctorate in Literature** by **Kennedy University, USA**.

His earlier books:

I Wish Someone Told Me This Before My First Job (2024)

Mindful Momentum: Navigating Procrastination and Overthinking (2025)

Dr. Rajput has been featured in **Forbes India (2025)** as a *Visionary Leader Influencing Society* and in **Fortune Magazine (India Edition)** for his work spanning leadership, authorship, and education. He has also been recognised among the **Top 10 Inspiring Personalities of 2025** by *India Today* and *Business Today*. His accolades include the **British Literary Award (2025)**, **National Icon Award (2025)**, **Rabindranath Tagore Literature Award**, **Asia's Most Promising Professional Skills Trainer & Inspiring Writer Award**, and the **Bharat Vibhushan Puraskar (2024)**.

With *Courage Within: Indian Tales of Grit and Values*, Dr. Rajput turns his focus toward the **Alpha Generation**, offering culturally rooted stories that nurture resilience, empathy, integrity, and character - reviving the spirit of a **modern-day Panchatantra** for today's readers. While written for young minds, the stories speak equally to adults who believe that values are lifelong companions.

When not writing or teaching, Dr. Rajput enjoys traveling, listening to everyday stories of perseverance and purpose - voices that quietly inspire the narratives he brings to life.

www.sushantrajput.com

Instagram: @dr_sushant_rajput3117

Table of Contents

No.	Story Title	Theme	Setting	
1	The Potter's Son	Grit in the face of poverty	Rural Rajasthan	01
2	Kavya and the Kite Festival	Handling failure with grace	Ahmedabad, Gujarat	08
3	The Lost Race	Grit and Determination	A tribal village in Koraput, Odisha	14
4	The Silent Warrior	Martial training for discipline	Kerala – Kalari village	20
5	The Banyan Tree Oath	Lesson in transparency and integrity	A village holding an ancient banyan tree in West Bengal	25
6	The Last Mile to School	Against all odds	Himaachal Pradesh's mountain village	31
7	Gopal and the Broken Tabla	Persistence in the pursuit of passion	Small town in West Bengal	35
8	The Village of One Light	Honour for tradition and knowledge	Rural Tamil Nadu	40
9	Arjun's Archery Test	Focus and mental discipline	Ancient Hastinapura Kingdom	44
10	The Secret of the Mango Seller	Trust is Only Built With Honesty	Busy market street in Pune	48
11	Shanthi's Second Chance	Learning from failure in classroom	Town in Andhra Pradesh	52
12	The Festival of Forgiveness	Respect and reconciliation	Village near Varanasi	57
13	Lalitha and the Long Summer	Grit during family hardship	Telangana countryside	61
14	The Honest Carpenter of Kashi	Character and Integrity	Kashi (Varanasi)	66

15	The Bullock Cart Race	Patience, Regularity and Country Dignity	Maharashtra countryside	71
16	Ravi's Red Mark Sheet	From flop to fire in the belly	A beautiful outskirt in Belagavi (Karnataka)	77
17	The Unseen Garden	Empathy and ethical choices	Botanical garden in Sikkim	82
18	My Father's Footsteps	Supporting a parent who is struggling	Chawl in Mumbai	87
19	The Rainy Day Resolution	Discipline in daily habits	Rainy morning in Udupi, Karnataka	92
20	The Sitar and the Street Boy	Talent grows with hard work	Street corner in Lucknow	97
21	A Letter to My Future Self	Values to live by	Diary entry across India	102
22	End Note: Why Stories Matter More Than Ever			106

STORY 1

THE POTTER'S SON

The village of Ranakpur baked under the Rajasthani sun. Its dusty lanes stretched between banyan trees whose roots twisted like old secrets into the earth. On the village's edge stood a small mud hut where Madho, the potter, lived.

Madho's hands were cracked and calloused, hardened by years of toil. Yet when they touched clay, they shaped more than pots, they shaped stories. His vessels carried water, grain, prayers, and dreams.

Madho owned little. His kurta was faded, his earnings meagre. But he held two treasures no drought could take away: hope, and his twelve-year-old son, Veer.

Veer was wiry, sun-kissed, and restless with imagination. Each dawn, before school, he kneaded lumps of wet clay beside his father, his small fingers pressing, shaping, learning. But while his hands molded earth, his eyes dreamed of stone and steel.

"Baba," he'd say, sketching with a stick on the dirt floor, tracing lines of walls and rooftops, "one day I'll build houses that don't leak when it rains."

Madho would chuckle, his tired eyes soft with pride. He'd ruffle his son's hair and reply, "Then you'll need more than bricks, beta. You'll need grit, a fire that never dies."

And silently, Veer promised himself that his fire would burn as long as it took.

Every day, Veer walked four kilometers to school. His bag cloth, frayed at the strap, slung over one shoulder. His cracked slippers slapped against the blistering road. He passed mustard fields glowing gold, cactus rows bristling like sentries, and children who waved barefoot from the lanes.

Inside his bag was no shiny tiffin, no polished pencil box. Just a rolled roti wrapped in cloth, and a hunger greater than hunger for food: a hunger for knowledge.

In class, Veer's eyes never wavered from the chalkboard. He borrowed torn books from older students. He scribbled notes on scraps of newspaper. At night, under the dim breath of a kerosene lamp, he solved sums on the mud walls of his hut.

He never complained. Not when kite festivals passed him by. Not when friends wore crisp new uniforms while he wore patched shirts. Not even when laughter trailed behind him like dust. Deep inside, Veer carried a stubborn belief: ***his dreams were bigger than his struggles.***

One morning, his teacher announced:

"A district-level scholarship exam is coming. The winner will earn admission to a city school, free of cost."

Gasps rippled through the classroom. For most, it was a distant dream. For Veer, it was a doorway.

"You should try," the teacher said, his gaze steady on Veer.

"But, Sir," Veer whispered, his throat dry, "I've never touched a computer. How can I compete?"

The teacher smiled. "A strong mind doesn't rely on tools. It relies on effort."

From that day, Veer became a boy on a mission. He sold his marbles and toy cart to buy a single new notebook. He gave up cricket matches. He gave up kite-flying. Every lunch break, he hovered over the school's only laptop, learning how the glowing screen worked, pressing its keys with cautious wonder.

At night, Madho often found him slumped over his notes, lantern dimming, chalk dust on his fingers.

The exam day arrived. Veer wore his father's cleanest shirt, pressed with care. His lunch, two rotis and a smear of pickle, was wrapped in banana leaves. On the bus to town, he pressed his face to the window as the desert melted into streets and buildings he had never seen before.

In the exam hall, rows of students in polished shoes and branded bags turned to look at him—the village boy with worn slippers. His heart pounded. He closed his eyes and whispered, "For Baba. For Ranakpur. For the dream."

And then he began to write.

Weeks later, the village waited like the desert waits for rain.

One evening, as goats returned home and the sun melted into dunes, a scooter rattled into the courtyard. The postman handed the schoolmaster a letter. Adjusting his glasses, the teacher read aloud:

"District Topper — Veer Madho."

Silence. For a breath, the village stood still. And then Ranakpur erupted. Drums beat. Children clapped. Neighbors hugged, some with tears streaming.

Madho stood frozen, clay still on his hands, before pulling Veer into his chest. His voice broke as he whispered, "You are not just my son... you are the pride of Ranakpur."

Many Years Later

The banyan trees still whispered, but Veer had changed. He returned not as a barefoot boy in patched clothes, but as a final-year engineering student with rolled blueprints tucked under his arm.

This time, he carried not just dreams, but designs.

With his guidance, the villagers built a community center—walls strong against storms, a roof that caught rain, solar lamps that lit up the night. Elders rested in its shade. Children's laughter filled its halls.

At the gate, Madho stood, his weathered face softened by tears and pride, watching Veer explain the building's design to curious neighbors.

"No leaks?" someone teased.

Veer smiled. "Not a single drop."

Beneath the same banyan trees where dreams were once drawn in dust, Veer had built not just walls, but hope.

Moral of the Story

Your background does not define your future. Grit and determination do.

Activities for Students

1. Build Your Grit Timeline

Draw a timeline of a goal you worked toward. Mark the moments you wanted to give up and how you kept going.

2. Design a Dream Village

Sketch or describe your ideal village or neighborhood. What would you build to make life better for everyone?

3. Interview Your Elders

Ask a parent or grandparent about a challenge they overcame. Share their story with the class, the way Veer's became Ranakpur's.

Reflection Questions

1. What made Veer different from the other students?
2. What sacrifices did he make for his dream?
3. How is grit different from talent?
4. Have you ever wanted to give up on something? What kept you going?
5. Why was the community center so meaningful for Veer?

Story 2

Kavya and the Kite Festival

The sky over Ahmedabad was alive with color. Red, blue, green, and gold. Thousands of kites battled in the wind, their strings cutting, clashing, and soaring. It was *Uttarayan*, the day when rooftops became battlegrounds and the sky turned into a festival of flying dreams.

But twelve-year-old Kavya wasn't on her terrace, cheering with the others. She sat in a corner, surrounded by broken kites and snapped strings, her hands clenched and her eyes brimming with unshed tears.

Just a week earlier, she had registered for her first junior kite-flying competition. Open to children between 10 and 15, it promised not just a gold medal but also a chance to fly alongside the state champion. Kavya had trained diligently every evening after school, practicing knots, learning the rhythm of the wind, and mastering the art of when to tug and when to glide.

Her father, a retired postman with gentle eyes and weathered hands, had given her his prized possession: an old wooden spool wrapped in crimson *manja*.

"You know," he had said with a nostalgic smile, "I never won a medal. But I never stopped flying. That's what matters."

On competition day, Kavya's heart raced as her kite soared into the sky. Higher and higher it climbed, slicing through the crowd of colors. For a shining moment, she was in the lead. She could almost see the medal around her neck.

And then, the wind shifted.

A sudden gust caught her off guard. Her grip loosened. The spool slipped. In a tangle of strings and paper, her kite nosedived into the crowd below. Gone.

Just like that, her dream came crashing down.

After the contest ended, Kavya sat apart, her shoulders slumped. She had trained, she had dreamed, and yet, she had nothing to show.

Her best friend Ananya knelt beside her. "Come on," she urged. "Let's go fly another one. Just for fun."

But Kavya shook her head, bitterness coating her words. "What's the point? I lost. Maybe I'm not meant for this."

At that moment, her father appeared. He wasn't holding a medal. He was holding a kite. A bright yellow, shaped like a bird in flight.

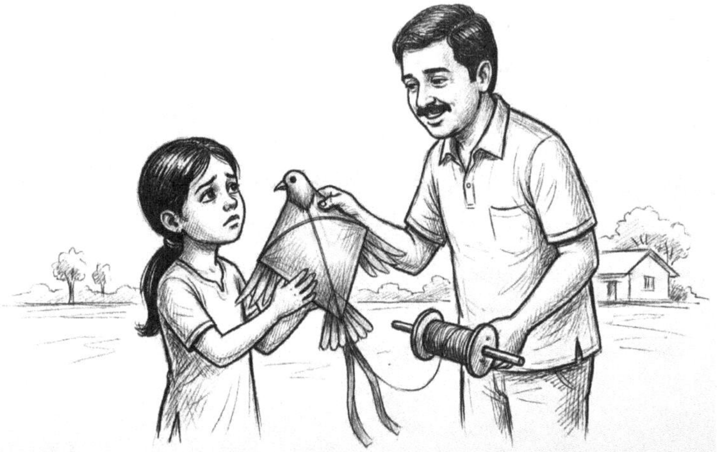

"Kites fall, beti," he said softly. "Even the best ones. But the wind..." He paused, letting her look at the sky. "...the wind never stops blowing."

Kavya followed his gaze. The sky above was still alive, kites darting, dipping, rising again. No one had stopped after losing a kite. They tied another and tried again.

Why should she be any different?

Wiping her eyes, Kavya took the yellow kite. This time there was no scoreboard, no judges, no pressure. Just her, her spool, and the endless sky.

She ran to the terrace edge and launched the kite upward. It caught the breeze instantly, soaring higher, dancing freely in the golden light. With each tug of the string, her confidence returned, thread by thread.

Down the street, she noticed a young boy struggling to free his kite caught in a tree. She jogged down, gently helping him untangle it. Handing it back, she smiled. "Next time, make the tail a little longer. It'll fly better."

That evening, when the kites were nothing but silhouettes against the sunset, Kavya opened her diary. In neat, careful letters she wrote:

"I didn't win the medal. But I learned to fly again."

One Year Later

On the next Uttarayan, the same terrace buzzed with laughter. Kavya, older now, stronger, with her hair whipping in the breeze, stood teaching a group of younger children. She showed them how to balance their spools, when to tighten the thread, when to let go.

She had become the mentor she once needed.

From the corner, her father sat cross-legged, sipping chai, watching his daughter with quiet pride. His eyes said everything words could not.

Moral of the Story

Failure is not the end. It is simply the wind changing direction. You adjust, and you learn to fly again.

Activities for Students

1. Kite of Courage Craft

Draw and decorate a kite. On it, write one failure you've learned from. Display them as a class "Sky of Comebacks."

2. Journal Prompt

Write a letter to your future self about a time you failed. What did you learn, and how would you face it differently next time?

3. Role Play

In pairs, act out a short skit. One student faces failure, the other helps them see the brighter side.

Reflection Questions

1. Why was the kite competition important to Kavya?
2. How did her father's words change her perspective?
3. What does the yellow kite symbolize?
4. Have you ever failed at something you cared about? What did you do next?
5. How can failure make us stronger?

Story 3

The Lost Race

The hills of Koraput were alive with whispers of rustling bamboo groves, of birds darting between jackfruit trees, of rain-soaked earth glowing red under the sun. In a small tribal village nestled in those hills lived Kuni, a spirited 13-year-old from the Kondh tribe.

Kuni was unlike the other girls in her village. While they spent their afternoons braiding flowers or painting tribal patterns on mud walls, Kuni's heart beat to a different rhythm. She loved to run.

Barefoot, across rice fields. Up the slopes. Through narrow forest trails. When her feet struck the earth, she felt weightless, free, as if the wind itself had chosen her as its companion.

But not everyone understood her gift.

At school in the nearby town, children mocked her. "You run like a jungle girl!"

"Where are your shoes, Kuni?"

She never replied. She simply smiled, tied her red ribbon tighter in her hair, and kept running.

One morning, the school announced the District Athletics Trials. Winners would be sent to Bhubaneswar for state-level training. For most students, it was a faraway dream. For Kuni, it felt like destiny calling.

Her coach, Mr. Singh, looked her up and down skeptically. "You? District trials?" He pointed at her dusty feet. "You've never even worn spikes." Kuni's gaze was steady. "No, sir. But I can run. Fast." The coach chuckled. "We'll see what your legs say on the track."

On race day, the contrast was striking. Girls from city schoo is arrived in branded jerseys, sleek shoes, and sparkling water bottles. Kuni wore a hand-stitched kurti, her hair tied back with that single red ribbon.

The whistle blew.

Kuni ran, not just with her legs, but with her heart. Each stride carried the rhythm of her village trails, the spirit of her hills. For three laps, she was in the lead. Victory seemed hers.

And then it happened.

Her foot caught on a small rock. She stumbled, crashed to the ground, her knee tearing open on the gravel. The others surged past. The finish line blurred as tears stung her eyes.

It was over.

Kuni sat at the edge of the field, clutching her bruised knee. Her chest heaved, not just with pain, but with something deeper.

Coach Singh walked over. "You had it... until the fall."

Kuni wiped her face, her voice soft but firm. "I still have it. I'm not done."

For the first time, the coach's expression softened. "If you train for six months, no excuses, no shortcuts, I'll take you to Bhubaneswar myself. No more trials. Do you have the grit?"

Kuni's answer was simple. "Yes, sir."

The next six months became a test of fire.

At dawn, while the village still slept, Kuni sprinted through the mist. She tied a tire around her waist and dragged it uphill. She lifted heavy stones. She squatted on slopes until her legs shook. Rain or shine, mud or heat, she never stopped.

The other girls whispered.
"She failed once. She'll fail again."
Kuni only smiled, knotting her red ribbon tighter.

Six months later, Bhubaneswar awaited. For the first time, Kuni stepped onto a synthetic track. The stadium roared with crowds. Flashing cameras caught every nervous face.

City athletes smirked when they saw her tribal kurti and plain shoes. But Kuni closed her eyes and imagined the red mud of Koraput beneath her feet, the sound of bamboo leaves rustling like applause.

The gunshot cracked.

She flew.

Her strides were fierce, graceful, unstoppable. This time there was no stumble, no rock, no fall. When she crossed the line, she had secured second place.

Coach Singh's eyes shone with pride. "You didn't win first, Kuni. But you proved something greater, you outran every doubt."

Years Later

Kuni went on to represent Odisha at national meets, her name etched among athletes who once doubted her. Yet, her favorite memory was not her medals or podium finishes.

It was that second-place race in Bhubaneswar, the day she discovered her true strength.

Because that was the day she won, even without coming first.

Moral of the Story

Grit is not about never falling. It is about rising every single time, stronger, faster, and more determined than before.

Activities for Students

Grit Journal – Write about one task you'll practice every day for a week, even when it's hard like waking up early or daily exercise.

Challenge Yourself Poster – Create a poster inspired by Kuni's journey with a motivational slogan about bouncing back.

Who's Your Kuni? – Think about a story of someone you know who kept going despite setbacks, a parent, teacher, or friend.

Reflection Questions

1. Why did people doubt Kuni?
2. What gave her the courage to keep going after her fall?
3. How would you define grit in your own words?
4. Can failure be part of success? Why?
5. What's something you gave up on—but want to try again?

Story 4

The Silent Warrior

In a quiet village near Kozhikode, where coconut palms swayed gently and temple bells echoed through the monsoon air, lived a boy named Aarav.

He was twelve, soft-spoken, thoughtful, and often lost in his own world. While other children laughed, argued, and played, Aarav sat by the lotus pond with a sketchbook in hand, tracing the wings of kingfishers or watching raindrops ripple across the water.

Many mistook his silence for weakness.

"He doesn't talk much," villagers whispered. "He's too gentle to survive in this world."

But they didn't know Aarav's secret.

Before dawn each morning, Aarav walked barefoot to a red-sanded pit- the Kalari, an ancient martial arts school.

There, under the watchful eye of Guru Rajan, he trained in Kalaripayattu, the oldest martial art of India. Aarav's body burned with effort. His arms ached from wooden sword drills. His legs trembled after horse stances. Yet he never complained.

One day, the Guru observed quietly before speaking: "You are like bamboo, Aarav. Quiet, but strong where it matters."

Aarav only nodded. For in Kalari, silence wasn't a weakness. It was strength. It was focus. It was respect- for the art, and for the self.

At first, his classmates teased him. They laughed when he stumbled during lion leaps or when his movements were slower than theirs.

But day by day, Aarav grew stronger. His steps became fluid. His breath controlled. His mind became sharper than before. Kalari didn't just shape his body, it disciplined his life.

He stopped wasting time in daydreams. He learned to rise early, eat mindfully, and sleep on time. Discipline became his quiet weapon.

One afternoon, the school announced a sparring event. Aarav was paired against Rohit, a boy known for his speed and strength.

The crowd murmured.

"Poor Aarav. He won't last a minute."

The bell rang.

Rohit charged, quick and forceful. Aarav didn't strike back immediately. He waited. His breathing was calm, his eyes steady. He remembered his Guru's words:

"A true warrior does not fight to defeat. He fights to understand."

Then Aarav moved- graceful, precise, like water slipping through stone. He deflected, dodged, and endured. He didn't overpower Rohit. He outlasted him.

When the match ended, silence hung heavy. Then the claps came, louder and louder. Rohit himself bowed deeply.

"I underestimated you," he admitted.

Aarav smiled softly. "That's all right. I used to underestimate myself too."

Months later, at the village festival, Aarav was invited to perform. Before the temple stage, he displayed his Kalari routine, his body flowing through stances with discipline and grace, his movements sharp yet controlled.

The crowd watched in awe. This was no timid boy. This was a warrior.

Aarav still sketched by the lotus pond. He still loved the sound of rain. But now, when he walked through the village, people no longer saw him as "too quiet." They saw him for what he truly was—calm, disciplined, unshakable.

Moral of the Story

True strength isn't loud. It is patient, disciplined, and rooted in self-respect.

Activities for Students

Discipline Diary Challenge – Keep a daily log of small habits (waking early, finishing homework, exercise). Reflect on how discipline changes your day.

Create Your Warrior Pose – Invent your own "warrior stance" and explain the value it represents- courage, focus, or resilience.

Traditional Arts Map – Research one traditional martial or performing art of India (like Kalari, Silambam, Gatka) and present it to the class.

Reflection Questions

1. Why did people think Aarav was weak in the beginning?
2. How did Kalari training change his mindset and habits?
3. What role does discipline play in building true strength?
4. Have you ever been underestimated? How did it feel?
5. What daily routines can help you stay disciplined?

Story 5

The Banyan Tree Oath

In Sundarpur, a peaceful village in West Bengal, there stood an ancient banyan tree. Its roots twisted deep into the earth, its branches stretched wide like a canopy of stories. For generations, the tree had been the heart of the village, where elders sipped chai, children played hide-and-seek, and meetings were held under its shade.

Among those children was Ishaan. Thirteen years old, quick-witted, and sharp with words, Ishaan was the boy everyone admired. He excelled at debates, charmed teachers with clever answers, and always found a way out of trouble. But sometimes, his cleverness bent the truth.

One day, the school announced a science project competition. The prize: a scholarship to a prestigious camp in Kolkata. Ishaan's eyes lit up with excitement, but dread followed. The deadline was only three days away, and he hadn't even begun.

That evening, at the tutoring center, Ishaan spotted his friend Rajat's model, a solar-powered windmill, carefully built, every blade turning in the breeze. Ishaan froze.

"What if I copied this? Just a few tweaks... no one will know."

The thought lingered. The next morning, Ishaan submitted a model eerily similar to Rajat's. The teachers were thrilled.

"Innovative work, Ishaan! Excellent design."

The applause rang in his ears, but so did Rajat's words from the day before: *"I worked for days on it... I hope I win this time."*

That night, guilt kept Ishaan awake. He stared at the project on his table, but all he could see was Rajat's disappointed face. Outside, the banyan tree stood tall, its branches whispering in the night breeze—as if watching him.

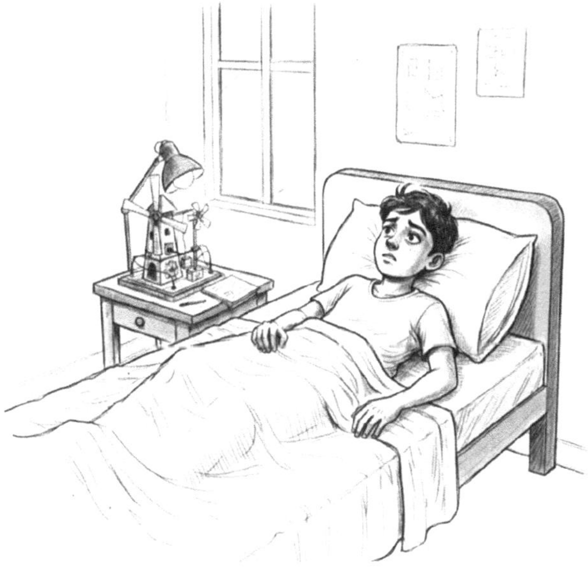

The next day, Rajat walked into class looking crushed. "Someone copied my project. The teachers think I cheated."

Ishaan's throat went dry. He ran to the banyan tree and sat beneath its roots, hiding from the world. Just then, the village priest passed by.

"This tree has heard both truths and lies for over a hundred years," the priest said gently. "It knows who's honest. But the real question is, do you?"

A gust of wind rustled the leaves. Ishaan knew what he had to do.

At the school assembly, just as the principal was about to announce the winner, Ishaan stepped forward. His heart pounded, but his voice was steady.

"Sir… I need to confess. The project wasn't mine. I copied it from Rajat. He deserves the credit."

The crowd gasped. The hall fell silent. Then the principal nodded with quiet respect.

"Honesty takes more courage than winning, Ishaan. Today, you showed true strength."

The applause this time wasn't for his cleverness, it was for his honesty.

That evening, Ishaan tied a red thread to the banyan's branch, a village tradition for solemn oaths. He whispered, "From today, no more lies. Only truth."

Tying the Oath

Ishaan grew up to be a respected civil servant, known for his fairness and integrity. People trusted his word as much as they trusted the old banyan tree, which still stood tall in Sundarpur-silent, strong, and proud.

Moral of the Story

Doing the right thing isn't always easy, but it's always right.

Activities for Students

The Truth Tree Pledge – Write one honest choice you've made (or wish you had) and pin it to a classroom "truth tree."

Build Your Moral Compass – Draw a compass with values like honesty, kindness, respect. Write how each guides you.

Reflection Questions

1. Why did Ishaan copy the project instead of making his own?
2. What made him confess at the assembly?
3. How would you feel if someone got credit for your work?
4. Is it ever okay to lie? Why or why not?
5. Can honesty after a mistake rebuild trust?

Story 6

The Last Mile to School

High in the misty hills of Himachal Pradesh, the village of Chandpur clung to a mountain slope. The air smelled of pine, and clouds often floated between the rooftops. Life was simple, but for 13-year-old Anmol, it wasn't easy.

There were no buses, no bookstores, not even an internet café. But Anmol had something more powerful than all of that- a fierce hunger to learn.

Mountain Path

Every morning, he wrapped his notebooks in a plastic sheet, slipped into his faded jacket, and began his seven-kilometer trek to school in Banjar.

He crossed two shaky wooden bridges, climbed slippery forest trails, and dodged stubborn mountain goats. By the time he

Bridge Crossing

reached school, his shoes were muddy, his hands red from the cold, but his smile never faded.

His classmates arrived in jeeps or on bicycles. They teased him for his torn bag and lunch wrapped in newspaper. But Anmol didn't mind. Every step through the mountains was a step toward his dreams.

One monsoon morning, the village pradhan warned, "The river is swelling. The bridges may break. Children must stay home."

But that day was special, it was exam day. The results would decide who won the state-level scholarship to a boarding school in Shimla, with free books, uniforms, and meals.

Anmol looked at the raging sky. Then he looked at his worn shoes. And he ran.

The path had turned into a stream. He slipped twice, bruised his knee once. The second bridge creaked under the roaring river below. At one point, his bag slipped from his hands,

Classroom Arrival

his books drenched with rain. His body shook with cold.

But he kept moving.

Exam Hall

Three hours later, soaked to the bone, Anmol stepped into the exam hall. The teacher gasped.
"You came through the storm?"

Anmol nodded, teeth chattering. "I studied too hard to let rain stop me."

Result Day

Weeks later, a letter arrived. Sealed with the Statc Education Board's emblem. The teacher read aloud: "Scholarship Winner – Anmol Thakur, Chandpur Village."

Tears blurred Anmol's eyes. For the first time, the last mile to school had carried him far beyond his mountains. His whole village erupted with pride.

Moral of the Story

Sometimes the longest journeys lead to the greatest destinations.

Activities for Students

Map Your Journey – Draw your daily journey to school and mark the challenges you face.

Determination Diary – Write about one time you didn't give up, even when it was difficult.

Reflection Questions

1. What challenges made Anmol's journey so difficult?
2. Why did he risk the storm for his exam?
3. What does his story teach us about determination?
4. Have you ever kept going when others gave up?
5. How do you think his village felt when he won the scholarship?

Story 7

Gopal and the Broken Tabla

In the small town of Krishnanagar, where sweet shops scented the streets with warm sandesh and rickshaw bells rang through the lanes, lived a boy named Gopal. He was twelve, with quick fingers that drummed on tabletops and tin cans as if the whole world were his instrument.

Music wasn't new to his family. Years ago, Gopal's grandfather had been a well-known tabla player. The old man's instrument, now worn and dusty, still rested on a shelf wrapped in red cloth. To Gopal, it wasn't just an heirloom, it was a silent invitation.

Krishangar Street View

One evening, as Gopal tapped spoons against bowls in rhythm with the radio, his mother chuckled. "You have Dadu's

Under the Banyan Tree

rhythm in your hands," she said. "It's time you learn properly."

So began his journey. Gopal joined Ustad Salim Khan's classes under the wide branches of a banyan tree. The other children came neatly dressed, their tablas gleaming. Gopal arrived with a patched schoolbag carrying his grandfather's old tabla.

He wasn't a prodigy. His beats slipped, his palms tired, and his classmates sometimes laughed. But Gopal kept showing up. After long evenings helping his father close the sweet shop, he would sneak upstairs, unwrap the tabla, and practice softly so as not to disturb his little sister.

Practice at Home

The town's annual music festival was fast approaching. Ustadji announced that the most dedicated student

The Broken Tabla

would perform on stage. Gopal's heart thudded- this could be his chance. He practiced before sunrise, skipped cricket games, and poured every ounce of energy into mastering the taal.

Then disaster struck. Days before the selection, his younger sister stumbled into the shelf while playing. The tabla crashed to the floor. Its skin tore; the sound was gone.

For a moment, so was Gopal's hope.

The next morning, he arrived at class empty-handed. "My tabla broke," he admitted quietly. Ustadji studied him. "And does that mean your practice is broken too?"

Shaking his head, Gopal whispered, "No, Ustadji. I practiced on the desk at home. Can I show you?"

He placed his palms on the wooden bench and began to play. Fingers rolled, tapped, and struck with precision, pulling rhythm from the lifeless wood. The other students fell silent, astonished. When he finished, Ustadji began to clap. Slowly, the rest followed.

At the festival, Gopal performed proudly, this time on a tabla borrowed from his teacher. His name was not only called as a performer, but as the boy whose music could not be broken.

Festival Performance

In the crowd, his father clapped with flour-dusted hands from the shop, while his little sister grinned widest of all.

Moral of the Story

True passion doesn't vanish with obstacles—it adapts, survives, and plays on.

Activities for Students

Passion Portrait

Draw or write about something you love. Share a time you almost gave up but didn't.

Sound Collectors

Spend five minutes listening carefully. List every sound you hear and share how even ordinary sounds can feel musical.

Reflection Questions

1. Why didn't Gopal stop practicing after his tabla broke?
2. How did he prove his passion to his teacher?
3. Have you ever found a creative way to continue something you love?
4. Why do you think Ustadji respected Gopal's bench performance?
5. What does Gopal's story teach us about resilience and passion?

Story 8

The Village of One Light

Veliyur was a tiny village in Tamil Nadu. Forty houses, one tea stall, one dusty road. But at its heart stood something special: a giant banyan tree. Every evening, the elders gathered under it, sipping tea and sharing stories.

Among them lived Meena, a bright twelve-year-old with curious eyes and bigger questions than anyone else in Veliyur. She wanted to be a scientist one day.

But there was one thing she couldn't figure out. Why did her whole village have just one streetlight?

Veliyur Village

The light stood near the banyan tree. Each night it flickered on, glowing softly over the circle of villagers.

"Why not add more lights?" Meena asked her father.

He laughed. "We've lived with one for years. It's enough."

"But we have temple funds!" she pressed. "We could light the whole street!"

Her father smiled. "Then ask Thatha. If he agrees, the village will too."

Thatha was the oldest man in Veliyur. His back was bent, but his mind was sharp as ever. That night, Meena marched up to him with her notebook.

"Thatha, look!" she said proudly. "I've drawn a plan for six more streetlights. We can afford it!"

Thatha leaned forward. "Why do you think we need more lights, child?"

"So children can play longer, people can walk safely, and no one will trip over cows!" she giggled.

Thatha chuckled, then grew serious. "All good reasons. But tell me—what happens when the whole street is bright? What do we lose?"

Meena blinked. "Lose? I don't understand."

"Long ago," Thatha said gently, "we had no bulbs. We had only the moon, the stars, and each other. This one light brings us together. It slows us down. It makes us listen. If the streets were full of lights, would anyone sit here? Or would they stay indoors, staring at screens?"

Evening Gathering

Meena looked around. Parents, children, farmers, shopkeepers, everyone was sitting together, their faces glowing under the single lamp. She felt quiet inside.

The next morning, she stood before her class with her plan. But instead of asking for streetlights, she said:

"Let's put small solar lanterns outside every house. Just enough to keep homes safe. But let's keep the single streetlight by the banyan tree. That way, our gathering will never fade."

Her classmates clapped. Her teacher's eyes shone with pride.

Presentation in Class

That evening, when Meena came home, Thatha was waiting with a lantern in his lap. "One light for your ideas," he said, handing it to her.

That night, Veliyur glowed brighter than ever. But under the banyan tree, the circle of stories still lived on.

Moral of the Story:

Wisdom isn't about adding more. Sometimes, it's about protecting what matters most.

Activities for Students:

Story Circle – In class, gather in a circle and share one story from your family or culture.

Light Journal – Write about a moment when you learned something important from an elder instead of a book.

Lantern Night

Reflection Questions:

1. Why did Meena first want more streetlights?
2. What lesson did Thatha teach her?
3. How did Meena change her plan?
4. Can technology and tradition live side by side?
5. What's one tradition in your community that you'd want to keep alive?

Story 9

Arjun's Archery Test

Many years ago, in the kingdom of Hastinapura, young princes were trained to become warriors. Among them was Arjun. He wasn't the tallest. He wasn't the strongest. But he had something rare, when Arjun focused, the whole world disappeared.

Their teacher was Guru Dronacharya, a strict and wise man whose eyes noticed everything. One bright morning, he called the princes and took them into the forest. The boys followed with their bows, whispering to each other. "Will it be a race?"

"Or maybe hunting?"

There was a tall tree. On its branch sat a wooden bird. Its eye was painted black.

"This," said Guru Drona, pointing to the bird's eye, "is your target today."

The princes looked at each other. A wooden bird? This seemed simple.

Drona called the first boy. "Yudhishthira, come forward."

Yudhishthira aimed his bow.

"What do you see?" Drona asked.

"I see the tree, the sky, the bird, and the branch," Yudhishthira answered.

"Put your bow down," Drona said.

One after another, the princes stepped forward. Some talked about the bird's feathers, some about the wind in the leaves. Every time, Drona shook his head.

Finally, it was Arjun's turn.

He walked up quietly, lifted his bow, and looked straight at the target.

"What do you see, Arjun?" Drona asked.

"I see only the eye of the bird," Arjun replied.

"Nothing else?"

"Nothing else, Guruji. Just the eye."

There was silence. Then Drona smiled. "Shoot."

Arjun's arrow flew fast, slicing the air. *Thwack!* It struck the wooden bird's eye perfectly.

The other princes gasped. Arjun lowered his bow calmly.

Later, by the river, his cousins crowded around him. "How did you do it?" they asked.

Arjun smiled. "I didn't look at anything else. Because whatever we focus on, that's what we hit."

Years later, Arjun became one of the greatest archers

the world had ever known. Not only because of his skill, but because of his focus. Even today, when someone gives their full attention to a goal, people say they have the focus of Arjun.

Moral of the Story:

True discipline begins in the mind. Focus turns practice into power.

Activities for Students:

Draw Your Target – Write a goal in the center of a target. Around it, write the distractions you need to ignore.

Reflection Questions:

1. What made Arjun different from the other princes?
2. Why did Drona stop the others but not Arjun?
3. When was the last time you lost focus on something important?
4. What little habits can help improve your concentration?
5. How can you use Arjun's lesson in today's noisy world?

Story 10

The Mango Seller's Secret

Pune's market lanes were always alive- cycle bells ringing, vendors calling out prices, and the air thick with the smell of spices and flowers. But under the shade of a big gulmohar tree stood a boy who quietly became the talk of the street.

His name was Sameer. He was only fourteen, yet he ran a mango cart all by himself. His father had fallen ill, so Sameer had taken charge. Each dawn, while most children still slept, he would ride to the wholesale yard, handpick Alphonso mangoes, and stack them neatly on his cart. By afternoon, his hands were sticky and his shirt yellow with pulp, but his smile never faded.

There was one thing that made Sameer different. He never cheated.

Other sellers sometimes hid rotten fruit at the bottom or used stones to increase weight. Sameer never did. He gave exactly what he promised.

People noticed.

A professor told her students, a watchman told his relatives, and slowly a whisper spread: "Buy from the boy under the gulmohar. He won't fool you."

One morning, a man in a starched kurta came to the cart. He picked up a mango and asked sharply, "Are these really fresh?"

"Yes, saab," Sameer replied. "Picked this morning."

The man narrowed his eyes. "And how do I know you're not lying?"

Without hesitation, Sameer reached under his cart and pulled out a small notebook. Inside were pages filled in his neat handwriting, dates, farm names, prices paid. His private ledger.

"You keep all this?" the man asked, surprised. "For myself," Sameer said softly. "But if you'd like to see, it's open. My father always told me your name is your true wealth."

The man closed the book, smiled, and paid for a dozen

mangoes. He didn't bargain.

A week later, Sameer was approached by a woman in a simple cotton saree. She introduced herself as Mrs. Mehra, the head of a well-known organic food brand.

"We're looking for honest suppliers," she said. "Would you like to sell at our weekend farmer's market?"

Sameer blinked in disbelief. "But I'm just a roadside seller."

She smiled. "No. You're trusted."

Months passed, and Sameer's little cart grew into a proper stall at the farmer's market—chalkboard prices, baskets of golden mangoes, and a framed photo of his father watching proudly over it all.

Yet whenever people visited, they still said, "Ah, it's the boy under the gulmohar."

And Sameer knew, his true sweetness was never just in the fruit. It was in the trust he offered.

Moral of the Story:

Honesty creates a reputation so strong, no one can steal it.

Activities for Students:

Trust Tree

Draw a tree. On the trunk, write "Trust." On each branch, list qualities that build trust (honesty, responsibility, fairness, etc.).

Run Your Own Market

Create a classroom activity where students "sell" items and have to make ethical decisions, do they tell the truth? Do they offer refunds?

Journal Prompt: What's Your Name Worth?

Ask students to write about how they want to be remembered by others, at school, at home, with friends.

Reflection Questions:

1. Why did Sameer gain a reputation in the market?
2. What made Mrs. Mehra trust him?
3. Have you ever done the right thing even when no one was watching?
4. How does honesty help build long-term success?
5. Why do you think people remembered Sameer as "the boy under the gulmohar"?

Story 11

Shanthi's Second Chance

In the leafy town of Rajahmundry, where the Godavari River shimmered in the morning sun, lived a quiet fourteen-year-old girl named Shanthi. She loved learning, could remember every fact, and had always been at the top of her class. Teachers admired her, neighbors compared, and even she felt the pressure to never slip.

But one day, life surprised her.

It was her science board exam. Shanthi had studied for weeks. Every diagram, every formula, every law of motion was in her head or so she thought. But as the question paper landed on her desk, her mind went blank. Her hands shook, her chest tightened, and letters danced across the page. She tried to write, guessed some answers, and left many blank.

Weeks later, the results arrived. She had failed.

The whispers began:

"She must have been overconfident."

"Maybe she isn't as smart as we thought."

Shanthi shut herself in her room. She ignored friends and even her younger brother quietly left food outside her door. Her parents didn't scold her, but they didn't know what to say either.

Then her grandmother came. She walked in carrying an old sewing kit and a worn book.

"When your grandfather lost his job," she said, "I stitched clothes to survive. I poked my own fingers over and over to learn it right." She looked at Shanthi warmly. "Failing isn't the end. It's just the middle of learning. You fell, that's all. Now get up and try again."

She handed Shanthi a science guide her father had used.

The next day, Shanthi went to the library. Heads turned, whispers followed, but she walked straight in. She borrowed books, watched online lessons, and joined a study group with other students retaking exams. She asked questions, practiced tirelessly, and refused to let pride or fear stop her.

When her re-exam came, she was calm, steady, and focused. She didn't top the class, but she passed with confidence.

Her teacher didn't praise the score that day. He praised Shanthi's courage. Because passing was just part of the story. Rising after failure, that was the real victory.

m that day on, Shanthi wasn't just a student, she was a fighter.

Moral of the Story:

Failing once doesn't define you. How you rise afterward does.

Activities for Students:

My Learning Curve – Draw a curve showing a time they struggled and how they improved. What helped them?

Failure Journal – Write about a time they failed, how it felt, and what they learned.

Letter to Myself – Write a note to their future self about facing setbacks with strength.

Reflection Questions:

1. Why did Shanthi fail even after preparing so well?
2. How did her grandmother's story change her thinking?
3. Why is it important to try again even if others doubt you?
4. Can failure ever be a gift? Why or why not?
5. What advice would you give a friend who failed at something important?

Story 12

The Festival of Forgiveness

In a small village near Varanasi, where the Ganga shimmered under the morning sun, the air smelled of incense and fresh marigold petals. Everyone was preparing for Kshama Parva, a festival of forgiveness, when villagers set aside pride and asked each other for pardon.

"Even the sun bows low before kindness," the elders would say.

But twelve-year-old Ritu was not ready to forgive.

She and her best friend Kesar had been inseparable, playing gilli-danda, making rangolis, and sharing mango pickle at lunch. But a week ago, something had come between them.

Ritu accused Kesar of tearing her drawing during the school art contest. Kesar denied it, but Ritu refused to listen.

"I saw your bracelet near my bag!" Ritu had shouted. "I dropped it while borrowing your sharpener!" Kesar had cried, eyes wide with hurt.

Since then, they hadn't spoken—at school, at the neighborhood, or even at the temple.

Now the village was glowing with the soft light of diyas. Children wore bright new clothes, elders sat beneath neem trees, writing names of those they wanted to ask forgiveness from. At sunset, each would approach the person, fold their hands, and say:

"Michhami Dukkadam" – meaning, *If I have hurt you in thought, word, or deed, knowingly or unknowingly, forgive me.*

Ritu stood at her doorstep, heart pounding. Her mother nudged her gently.

"You know what to do, beta."

Ritu bit her lip. "But what if she never forgives me?"

"Forgiveness is not about control," her mother said softly. "It's about courage."

As temple bells rang, Ritu walked through the narrow lanes toward the ghat. Her palms were sweaty, her voice trapped in her throat. She spotted Kesar lighting a diya by the river.

Their eyes met. Silence wrapped around them like morning mist.

"I was wrong," Ritu whispered. "I judged you without knowing the truth. I was hurt and didn't listen."

Kesar's lip trembled. "I should have explained better. I was scared... but I never wanted to hurt you."

They stood still. Then, without another word, Kesar held out her hand. Ritu took it.

The diya flickered between them—soft, steady, forgiving.

That night, as the village floated lanterns down the Ganga, Ritu and Kesar stood side by side. Their diya floated ahead of the others, carving a path of light across the dark water.

Moral of the Story:

Forgiveness is a bridge we build, not for others to cross, but for ourselves to heal.

Activities for Students:

Forgiveness Flower – Draw a flower. On each petal, write the name of someone you want to forgive or ask forgiveness from. Share why it matters.

Role Play: The Apology Game – Practice apologizing and responding with grace through real or imagined situations.

Letter of Peace – Write a short letter to someone (even if you don't send it) expressing forgiveness or asking for it.

Reflection Questions:

1. Why was it hard for Ritu to apologize?
2. What made Kesar forgive her?
3. Have you ever said sorry when it was really difficult?
4. How does it feel when someone forgives you?
5. Can a community become stronger by practicing forgiveness?

Story 13

Lalitha and the Long Summer

In the sun-baked countryside of Telangana, where the soil cracked and the wind smelled of dust, lived thirteen-year-old Lalitha. Her home was a small mud house surrounded by dry fields, with a lone neem tree swaying lazily in the hot breeze.

Lalitha was clever, full of jokes, and dreamed of becoming a teacher. Every afternoon, she would line up her little cousins under the mango tree and teach them letters drawn in the dirt.

"Miss Lalitha!" they would call, giggling.

But that summer, life became hard.

Her father, a daily wage laborer, had fallen at a construction site and injured his leg. He couldn't work. Her mother's stitching orders were slow. Bills piled up. The kitchen was quiet. The rice jar emptied too quickly.

One evening, Lalitha overheard her parents speaking in hushed tones.

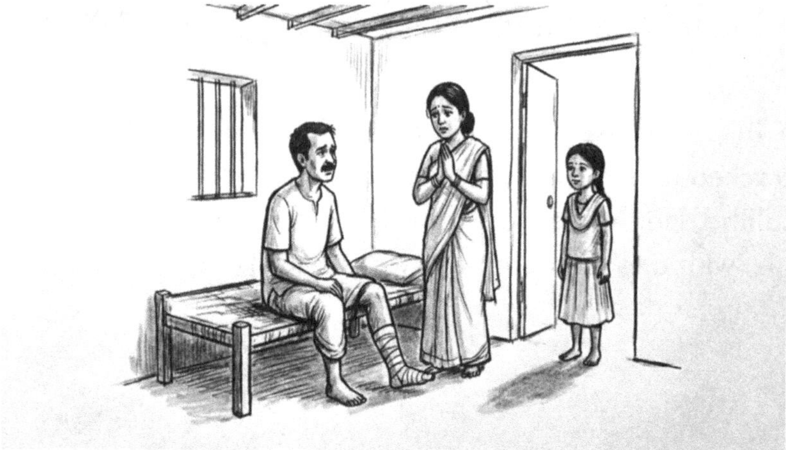

"No new notebooks this year," her mother whispered. "We might have to pull her out of school," her father said, his voice heavy.

Lalitha felt a tight knot in her chest. She didn't cry or shout. That night, lying on the cool floor under a rusted fan, she made a promise to herself.

"I will not give up. Not now."

The next morning, while her mother was away, Lalitha slipped into her old uniform and went to the village market. She asked every vendor if they needed help—carrying bags, cleaning stalls, sorting produce.

Most shook their heads. But one kind vendor finally said, "You can sweep and pack tamarind. I'll give you twenty rupees a day."

From that day, Lalitha worked in the market each morning. She tied back her hair, rolled up her sleeves, and carefully packed tamarind. Then she rushed to school, hands still smelling of sour pulp, sitting straight and answering every question.

Her teachers were amazed.

"But you're already our top student," one whispered. "I still am," she said quietly, smiling.

Weeks passed. Then one day, the headmaster called her in.

"Lalitha," he said kindly, "a local trust heard your story. They're offering you a full scholarship for books, school supplies, and tuition."

Tears filled Lalitha's eyes. For the first time in weeks, she let herself breathe.

That night, her father sat under the stars, a cup of tea in hand, leg bandaged. He looked at her and said, "You held this family together."

Lalitha didn't reply. She just hugged him tightly.

Sometimes, the strongest pillar in a house is the one still in uniform.

Moral of the Story:

True grit isn't loud. It's the quiet strength that refuses to break.

Activities for Students:

My Resilience Story – Write or draw a time you had to push through a tough situation.

Daily Grit Tracker – Create a one-week journal tracking moments when you stayed strong during challenges.

Who Keeps Us Going? – List people who support you in hard times. What qualities make them strong?

Reflection Questions:

1. What motivated Lalitha to keep going even when things got hard?
2. How did her actions help her family?
3. What would you have done in her place?
4. Can small actions (like packing tamarind) make a big impact? How?
5. Who in your life shows quiet strength like Lalitha?

Story 14

The Honest Carpenter of Kashi

In the winding lanes of Kashi, the oldest city in the world, temple bells rang with the clatter of boat oars and the soft tap of hammers on wood.

At the end of a narrow alley behind Dashashwamedh Ghat, a quiet carpenter named Hari ran a small shop. His shop had no sign, no flashy displays, just a wooden bench, a rusty toolbox, and a half-finished rocking chair in the corner. But everyone in the neighborhood knew two things about Hari: his furniture was beautiful, and his word was unbreakable.

One summer, a wealthy zamindar from Lucknow came to Kashi to renovate his ancestral home.

"I need a bed, two chairs, and a cupboard," he said, handing Hari a thick envelope. "Here's half the payment. I'll pay the rest when I return. I don't need a receipt, I trust you."

Hari nodded quietly, tucked the envelope safely away, and began his work.

He picked the finest teak, carved patterns inspired by the ghats, and polished each piece until it shone like the Ganga at sunrise.

But as the final week approached, news arrived—the zamindar had died suddenly on his journey back.

The neighbors whispered, "Keep the furniture. Sell it. No one will ever know."

Hari said nothing. He wrapped each piece carefully, tied them with rope, and stacked them in a corner.

"For whom?" asked his apprentice.

"For the man who trusted me," Hari replied. "His family may come later, or maybe never. But his word matters more than coins."

Months passed. Seasons changed.

One winter morning, a little boy walked into the shop. He held a faded letter.

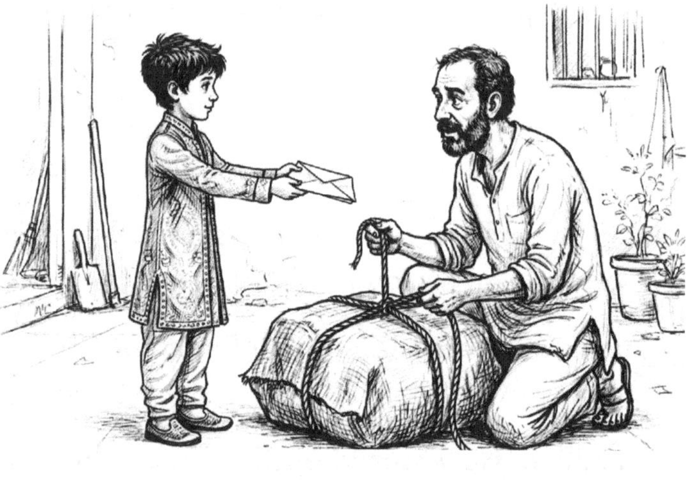

"Are you Hari-ji? My grandfather wrote about you in his will. He said, 'One man in Kashi still keeps his word.'"

Tears filled Hari's eyes. He untied the cloth wraps to reveal the furniture, which were untouched, shining, waiting.

The boy's eyes widened. "You didn't sell it?"

"No," said Hari, "because character is built in silence."

That day, as the boy and his father loaded the furniture, the lane watched in quiet admiration. From then on, whenever people in Kashi spoke of trust, they didn't mention temples or trade—they spoke of Hari, the man who did the right thing even when no one was looking.

Moral of the Story:

Integrity is what you do when no one is watching. It speaks louder than words.

Activities for Students:

Character Building Chart – List actions that show integrity and write examples from your own life.

Story Reimagining – Write what might have happened if Hari had sold the furniture. How would things change?

Silent Hero Poster – Design a poster for someone who quietly does the right thing—like a bus driver, librarian, or janitor.

Reflection Questions:

1. Why didn't Hari sell the furniture?
2. What do you think he gained by keeping his promise?
3. Have you ever done the right thing even when no one noticed?
4. Why is honesty important, even when no one is watching?
5. Who do you admire for their integrity or honesty?

Story 15

The Bullock Cart Race

In the green fields of rural Maharashtra, where sugarcane swayed with the wind and tractors hummed far away, the annual village fair of Nandgaon was everyone's favorite time of year.

There were food stalls, folk dances, wrestling matches, but the most awaited event was the legendary bullock cart race.

Farmers from nearby villages polished their carts, groomed their bullocks, and gathered at the dusty track. This race wasn't just about winning, it was about honor, pride, and keeping a tradition alive.

This year, for the first time, a boy named Vikram would run with a cart of his own.

Vikram was fifteen, thin but strong, with eyes that seemed to hold fire. His father had raced for years but was now too old to handle the reins. The family's pride rested on Vikram.

The villagers whispered, "Too young. Too inexperienced."

But Vikram remembered every lesson his father had taught him: how to whisper to the bullocks, oil the wooden wheels, and tighten each knot carefully.

So, he prepared. Every morning before sunrise, he ran barefoot beside the cart, fed the bullocks by hand, and polished the wood until it gleamed like the morning sun.

Other boys laughed. "You'll be thrown off the first turn!"

Vikram didn't answer. He just kept working.

Race day arrived. The track was dusty and uneven. The sun beat down. Flags fluttered. Villagers cheered from both sides. Twenty carts lined up.

Vikram gently placed his hand on his bullock's forehead. "We run together, like always," he whispered.

The whistle blew. Dust flew. Some carts shot ahead, wobbling and rattling. But Vikram stayed calm. He didn't whip. He didn't shout. He let his bullocks find their pace.

Halfway through, others began to stumble—one cart toppled, another's bullocks grew tired. But Vikram moved steadily, urging them gently.

In the final stretch, his team surged ahead, strong and focused. He crossed the finish line, not first, but third.

The crowd erupted, clapping as if he had won gold.

An old man approached him. "You didn't just race," he said, patting Vikram's shoulder. "You showed us why this tradition matters."

That night, as lamps glowed and music filled the air, Vikram sat beside his bullocks, feeding them jaggery and stroking their ears.

He hadn't won gold, but he had earned something even greater: respect.

Moral of the Story:

Rushing might get you ahead, but patience, persistence, and care take you farther.

Activities for Students:

Patience Challenge – Give a task requiring slow, steady effort, like stacking blocks or building a small structure, then reflect on the process.

Local Traditions Collage – Collect or draw pictures of traditions that require patience, like kolam, kite flying, or folk dances.

Respect in Action – Discuss how Vikram treated his bullocks. Ask students to list ways they show respect to animals, people, and traditions.

Reflection Questions:

1. Why didn't Vikram rush during the race?
2. How was his approach different from the other racers?

3. How can patience help in real-life challenges?

4. Can you think of something in your life that requires daily effort?

5. Why is it important to preserve traditions while growing as individuals?

Story 16

Milind's Red Mark Sheet

On the outskirts of Belagavi, Karnataka, a government school woke up to the morning bell. Dust swirled in the sunlit corridors as students shuffled to their classrooms, books clutched tight, whispering guesses about the day's test results.

In the back row sat Milind, a boy with messy hair, scuffed shoes, and eyes that rarely met anyone else's. He wasn't the class clown or the rebel as he was invisible in the eyes of most.

That morning, the teacher entered with a stack of mark sheets. Names were called one by one. Some students raced up eagerly, while Milind waited, palms sweaty. Finally, his name rang out.

He walked to the front, took his sheet, and returned to his bench without looking.

Later, behind the cycle shed, he unfolded the paper. The numbers glared at him in red: 25 out of 100.

Failed. Again.

He crumpled the sheet, stuffed it into his pocket, and turned to leave. That's when he heard the whispers:

"Why does he even come to school?"
"Bet he'll drop out by high school."
"Red mark Milind!"

The laughter stung more than the marks.

He walked home slowly. His parents, tired from daily labor, didn't ask about the results. They were used to disappointment.

That night, Milind stared at the red numbers. And then something inside him shifted.

The red ink didn't scare him—it challenged him.

He smoothed out the sheet, grabbed his notebook, and opened his math book. Page one.

For the next few weeks, Milind did what he had never done before.

He arrived early at school and asked the topper, Meena, for help. Surprised, she agreed. He stayed late, solving problem after problem. He borrowed books, watched lessons on a neighbor's phone, and wrote essays in old notebooks. Slowly, the numbers that had once made no sense began to form patterns. Mistakes lessened. Confidence grew.

In the final exam of the year, Milind didn't come first. Not even in the top ten. But he scored **62 out of 100.**

It wasn't red ink anymore—it was blue. And next to the number, the teacher had written a single word: **"Improved."**

At the school assembly, his name was called for the "Most Improved Student" award. Milind couldn't believe it. But as applause rang through the hall, he realized something powerful: he hadn't just passed a test, he had passed the point of giving up.

From that day on, whenever he faced a hard problem, he didn't run. He looked it in the eye and said quietly: **"Page one."**

Moral of the Story:

Failure is not the end, it's the starting point of determination.

Activities for Students:

Progress Graph – Chart improvement in a subject or skill over time. Celebrate small wins.

Red to Blue Reflection – Write or draw about a "red mark" moment and how you overcame it.

Peer Tutoring Day – Pair students as tutor and learner to help each other improve.

Reflection Questions:

1. What made Milind change his view of failure?
2. Why is asking for help a sign of strength, not weakness?
3. Have you ever improved at something with practice? How did it feel?
4. What matters more—being the best or trying your best?
5. How can we support classmates who are struggling instead of teasing them?

Story 17

The Unseen Garden

In the misty hills of Sikkim, behind the government school and framed by blooming rhododendrons, there was a quiet place no one really talked about, but everyone knew. It was called the Unseen Garden.

A signboard marked it. Just an old wooden gate, slightly open, with vines curling like lazy fingers. Most students walked past without noticing.

Except for Aarav.

Aarav was twelve, naturally curious, quietly observant. While other kids rushed home after school, he lingered watching ants march, sketching birds, wondering how clouds could float yet carry water.

One day, chasing a butterfly, he wandered through the gate. His eyes widened.

Inside were dozens of plants - some in pots, some in carefully dug beds. Lemongrass, basil, rare ferns, wild strawberries. In the center stood a faded green bench and a rusted watering can.

But there was no gardener. Only footprints.

The next day, and the day after, the garden seemed cared for—soil freshly turned, dry leaves swept away.

"Who takes care of this?" Aarav asked his science teacher.

She smiled. "No one officially. Maybe someone with a green heart."

Intrigued, Aarav decided to find out.

That Saturday, he hid behind a tree at dawn. At 6:15 AM, an old man with a limp walked in, carrying a cloth bag. His sweater was worn, sandals tied with rope. He moved slowly—but his hands were gentle.

He watered the plants, whispered to them, even played a tiny flute as he worked.

Aarav followed him discreetly and discovered that he was Uncle Norbu, the school's retired gardener. No salary. No recognition. Just love for the garden.

The following week, Aarav arrived early with a gift—new gloves and a packet of seeds.

"Why?" asked Norbu, surprised.

"You care for this garden without being asked. I want to help," Aarav said.

From that day on, the two worked together. Aarav learned to prune, compost, and even talk to plants as if they were friends.

One afternoon, Aarav saw a group of kids picking flowers to decorate the school gate.

"Hey!" he called. "These plants aren't just for decoration—they're someone's daily care!"

The kids laughed. "Who cares? It's just a garden."

"It's not just anything," Aarav said firmly. "Respect what's not yours."

The next morning, the same boys returned—not with teasing, but with water bottles and soil. Silently, they helped replant what they had picked.

At the year-end assembly, the headmistress called Aarav to the stage.

"For reminding us that caring begins quietly. And ethics aren't taught—they're practiced."

He turned to Uncle Norbu in the audience. "This garden will now officially be named The Green Heart Corner. And you, Norbu-ji, are its eternal caretaker."

The garden, once unseen, had become a symbol—of quiet work, small kindnesses, and the courage to protect what others ignore.

Moral of the Story:

Doing the right thing often starts when no one's watching - but it inspires everyone when they do.

Activities for Students:

Silent Acts of Care – Draw or write about a kind act you did when no one was watching. How did it make you feel?

Design Your Garden – Create a dream garden on paper. What plants grow there, and what does it stand for?

Ethical Choices Role Play – Act out situations where you must make the right decision when no one is looking.

Reflection Questions:

1. Why did Uncle Norbu care for the garden without recognition?
2. What did Aarav learn by observing him?
3. Why is it powerful to do good things quietly?
4. How did Aarav change the other students' perspective on the garden?
5. What is something you care about deeply, even if no one else notices?

Story 18

My Father's Footsteps

In the bustling city of Mumbai, where trains never sleep and the sea whispers stories to skyscrapers, lived fourteen-year-old Rohan.

He stayed with his parents in a one-room chawl—a narrow tenement shared with three other families. Clotheslines crisscrossed the hallway. The air smelled of frying onions, incense, and damp clothes. It was loud. It was cramped.

But it was home.

Rohan loved two things: cricket and sketching shoes.

Not ordinary shoes. Dream shoes - with flames, wings, neon

edges. He drew them on the backs of notebooks, old bills, even on the wall behind his bed (until his mother found out).

"I'll be a shoe designer one day," he would say confidently. His father, Suraj, would smile quietly and nod.

Suraj worked as a security guard in a high-rise building. He wore the same pale blue uniform every day and worked twelve-hour shifts. He left before sunrise and returned after dark—always tired, always kind.

One Sunday, Rohan's school hosted career day. Students were asked to bring their parents to speak about their work.

Rohan fidgeted with his pencil all week. Everyone else's parents were doctors, engineers, managers. He hesitated. "What will I say about Papa?"

When the day arrived, Suraj polished his shoes, ironed his uniform, and walked beside Rohan to school. Rohan kept glancing at his father's scuffed shoes and calloused hands.

On stage, one by one, students spoke. Then it was Rohan's turn.

He walked up slowly.

"This is my father, Suraj. He is a security guard. Every day, he stands outside while others enter big buildings. But he's the reason I can dream about entering them someday—not as a guard, but as a designer. He guards buildings. But more importantly, he guards my dreams."

There was silence. Then applause.

That evening, Rohan and his father sat on the terrace, legs dangling over the edge, as the city lights blinked below.

"I don't say it much," Rohan murmured, "but I notice everything. The double shifts. Walking in rain. Skipping meals just to buy me a new pencil box..."

Suraj looked at him, eyes moist.

"Walk wherever you want in life," he said softly. "Just remember whose feet walked the road before you."

Years later, Rohan didn't just design shoes. He launched a label called "Suraj Steps"—inspired by the quiet strength of the man who gave him everything without asking for anything in return.

Moral of the Story:

The strongest foundation for your future is often built on the silent sacrifices of those who came before you.

Activities for Students:

Walk in Their Shoes – Interview parents or guardians about their work. What sacrifices have they made? What lessons have they taught?

Design with Meaning – Create a design (shoe, bag, building) dedicated to someone you admire.

Gratitude Letter – Write a letter to a family member who inspires you, even if you never send it.

Reflection Questions:

1. Why did Rohan feel nervous about bringing his father to career day?
2. What changed after he introduced him?
3. What kinds of sacrifices did his father make for the family?
4. How can we show respect and gratitude to our parents or elders?
5. Who in your life has quietly supported your dreams?

Story 19

The Rainy Day Resolution

The coastal town of Udupi, Karnataka, was famous for its serene temples—and for sudden, heavy rainstorms. One moment the sky would be blue; the next, it would pour as if the clouds had been holding their breath for weeks.

Twelve-year-old Sharath loved the rain. He loved how it made the roads shiny and the trees sway. But there was one thing he didn't love—waking up early, especially during the monsoon.

Each evening, he promised himself he'd rise at 6:00 AM to jog with his uncle, a retired army man who believed, "Discipline is the first step to greatness."

And each morning, when the alarm rang, Sharath snoozed it once... twice... then rolled over.

One Monday, it rained harder than usual. Thunder growled. Streets flooded ankle-deep. Sharath sighed—surely his uncle would cancel today's jog.

But then—knock knock.

His uncle appeared at the door, raincoat on, umbrella in hand.

"Let's go, cadet!" he said.

"But... it's pouring!" Sharath stammered.

His uncle smiled. "Discipline doesn't wait for the weather."

Sharath groaned but got dressed, grumbling all the way.

The roads were slippery. His shoes soaked. Rain lashed his face like cold cloth.

"This is silly," he muttered.

But his uncle didn't lecture him. Instead, he shared stories—about waking up for drills in snow, soldiers marching with blisters, and how routine isn't about comfort—it's about commitment.

The next morning, Sharath woke up before the alarm. He slipped on his shoes, grabbed his raincoat, and stepped out.

His uncle raised an eyebrow. "Early today?"

Sharath shrugged. "One day won't make me disciplined. But one more day might help."

And so it began. Rain or shine, sleepy or sore, Sharath showed up.

At first, his legs ached. Then, they adjusted.

At first, he counted minutes. Then, he counted laps.

A month later, his class had a fitness test. Sharath surprised everyone—including himself—by finishing first in the long run.

His teacher clapped. "What changed?"

Sharath smiled. "One rainy day. One choice."

That year, Sharath didn't just grow stronger—he grew steadier. And every time he faced a challenge, he remembered: discipline isn't loud or heroic. It's the quiet habit of showing up—especially when it's inconvenient.

(Not sure why the boy suddenly looks all grown up in the above illustration)

Moral of the Story:

Discipline doesn't begin when it's easy. It begins when it's hard—and you still choose to show up.

Activities for Students:

Daily Habit Tracker – Track one small daily habit for a week (waking up, reading, stretching).

Discipline Stories – Share or write about someone who sticks to a routine despite challenges.

Rainy Day Journal Prompt – Write about a day you didn't want to do something but did it anyway. How did it feel afterward?

Reflection Questions:

1. Why didn't Sharath want to jog at first?
2. What helped him change his habit?
3. How can discipline help in school or at home?
4. What small daily habit would you like to build?
5. Why is it important to stay consistent, even when conditions aren't perfect?

Story 20

The Sitar and the Street Boy

In the heart of Lucknow, where the smell of kebabs mixes with the rhythm of kathak and every street corner tells a story, lived a boy named Faheem.

He had no fixed home. He slept under a cloth canopy beside a paan shop. His clothes were torn, his sandals mismatched. But his eyes sparkled with a secret: he had fallen in love—with a sitar.

Every evening, outside the music school on Nawab Road, he sat on the footpath, chin resting on his knees, listening. Inside, students practiced ragas and scales. Sometimes the notes floated out of the open windows like birds in flight. Faheem listened so intently that he could hum the entire piece by the time it ended.

One day, the music teacher stepped outside, and Faheem shyly said, "That was Raag Yaman, right, sir?"

The teacher paused. "How do you know that?"

"I hear it every day," Faheem smiled.

"You don't just hear it," the teacher said. "You feel it."

Faheem began sweeping the front steps of the school in exchange for leftover snacks and the chance to sit by the window. He picked up words like aalap, taal, and meend just by listening.

One evening, a student left their sitar behind. After everyone had gone, Faheem crept in and touched it carefully, as if it were made of glass. He plucked a string. Then another. The sitar sang.

The next morning, the teacher found Faheem sitting cross-legged, eyes closed, gently playing the scale.

"You've never had a lesson?" he asked.

Faheem shook his head. "Only the ones your windows gave me."

From that day on, the teacher gave him ten minutes a day with the school's old sitar. Ten minutes became twenty. Twenty became an hour. Faheem practiced harder than anyone. While other boys went home to play, he stayed behind, repeating the same note until it became part of his breath.

Months passed. The teacher saw something rare—not just talent, but discipline. He entered Faheem in a local competition for underprivileged children. "No pressure," he said. "Just play like the street is listening."

On competition day, Faheem wore a borrowed kurta, sat cross-legged on the stage, and closed his eyes. When he played, the audience fell silent. His music didn't just fill the hall—it filled hearts.

(he is supposed top be wearing a kurta, sat cross-legged on the stage, and closed his eyes)

He won. Not just the competition, but also a full scholarship to the music school. A sponsor offered him his own sitar, and the local newspaper ran a headline: "From the Streets to the Stage: The Boy Who Learned Through a Window."

Years later, Faheem didn't just become a performer. He became a teacher, opening a free evening class for children like him—who had nothing but curiosity and a good ear.

On the wall of that tiny classroom hung his first sitar, with a plaque that read:

"Talent is a seed. But only hard work makes it sing."

Moral of the Story:

Your talent opens the door. But it's your effort that lets you walk through it.

Activities for Students:

My Window to the World – Ask students what they've learned just by observing or listening. What inspires them from a distance?

Talent vs. Practice Chart – Make two columns: natural talents and skills that need practice. What helped you grow?

Reflection Questions:

1. What made Faheem's love for the sitar special?
2. How did he learn even without formal lessons?
3. What role did his teacher play in his journey?
4. Why is practice important even when you have talent?
5. Who is someone in your life who works hard quietly, like Faheem?

Story 21

A Letter to My Future Self

Dear Future Me,

I don't know where you are right now—maybe in college, starting your first job, or chasing a dream I can't even imagine yet. But today, I'm twelve years old, sitting by the window of our house in Belagavi (Karnataka), watching the rain tap softly against the glass. I'm writing this letter not because someone told me to, but because there are some things I hope you never forget.

Remember the day you lost the elocution contest? Not because you lost—but because you forgot your lines halfway and felt like you had disappointed everyone. Amma said something then, something you must hold on to forever: "Winning is a moment. Courage is a habit."

I hope you still try. I hope you still get up, even when you feel small or scared.

Remember the time you helped your classmate pick up his books after others teased him? You didn't know it then, but he told you later it was the first time someone had stood up for him. "Kindness doesn't need an audience." Please be kind—even when no one's watching. Even when it's easier not to be.

Remember the day you skipped a cricket match to help Appa clean the storeroom? He didn't say much, but later he fixed the zipper on your school bag without a word.

"Love isn't always loud. It's often found in quiet effort." Notice these moments. They're everywhere if you look closely.

You once wanted to be a teacher, then a detective, then a stand-up comedian. I hope you still dream, even if your path looks nothing like you expected. Just don't forget:

"It's okay to change your goals, as long as your values stay rooted."

Future Me, I hope you've made mistakes—yes, mistakes! Because that means you've tried. But I hope you also learned, grew, and forgave yourself. And above all, I hope you've stayed honest. Honest to others. Honest to yourself.

With love,
Your 12-year-old self
Trying. Learning. Growing.

Moral of the Story:

Sometimes, the best guide in life is the person you once were—before the world told you who to be.

Activities for Students:

Write Your Own Letter – Ask students to write a letter to their future selves about what they hope to learn and become.

Value Reflection Chart – List personal values like honesty, kindness, courage, and patience. Ask students to rate how well they live them today.

Time Capsule Project – Draw or write items to "store" in a mental time capsule—things they hope to keep as they grow.

Reflection Questions:

1. Why is writing a letter to your future self powerful?
2. Which parts of your personality do you hope never change?
3. What values do you want to carry with you forever?
4. How do small daily actions reflect bigger values?
5. If you opened this letter in 10 years, what would you want it to remind you of?

Closing Note

Why Stories Matter More Than Ever

In a world moving faster than ever, where attention spans are shrinking, screens are glowing brighter, and information comes at lightning speed, how do we help children truly learn, reflect, and grow?

The answer is simple: stories.

Not just any stories, but ones that speak their language, mirror their lives, and carry messages that don't preach, but reach.

This book was never meant to be a list of lessons. It was meant to be both a mirror and a map. A mirror to help young readers see themselves in the characters, their choices, and their journeys. And a map to gently guide them toward values they can carry into life- honesty, resilience, courage, empathy, and discipline.

For today's children, born into a world of instant information, smart devices, and endless content, traditional lessons often feel dull. But give them a well-told story, and you'll see their eyes widen, their minds wander, and their hearts open.

Stories wrap life lessons in adventure, ethics in emotion, and values in voice. They don't force children to remember, they help them feel, and when they feel, they remember naturally.

When a child reads about a village boy rising through grit, or a girl learning strength in failure, they aren't just reading, they are living the experience. And that is where real learning begins.

I chose storytelling not because it's easy, but because it is timeless. It worked when my grandmother told me bedtime stories. It works now, in pages like these. And it will continue to work, even in an AI-powered future, because stories speak the language of the human heart.

To every parent, teacher, mentor, and reader, know this: A story told at the right moment can do what a hundred lectures cannot.

It can shape a mindset, ignite a value, and guide a child through choices that truly matter.

Thank you for reading. Thank you for believing. And thank you for keeping the **power of storytelling alive**.